For Kim and Abbey.
—J.S.

To:
Sukey, as always, my real audience.

Nancy and Tracey, who gave me
my first glimpse of parenthood up close.

Jerry, friend and partner.
—R.K.

A BABY BLUES® TREASURY
THE SUPER-ABSORBENT BIODEGRADABLE FAMILY-SIZE BABY BLUES

BY RICK KIRKMAN & JERRY SCOTT

Andrews McMeel
Publishing

Kansas City

Other Baby Blues® Books from Andrews McMeel Publishing

Guess Who Didn't Take a Nap?
I Thought Labor Ended When the Baby Was Born
We Are Experiencing Parental Difficulties . . . Please Stand By
Night of the Living Dad
I Saw Elvis in My Ultrasound
One More and We're Outnumbered!

www.andrewsmcmeel.com

ISBN: 0-8362-3657-2

Library of Congress Catalog Card Number: 97-71637

CONTENTS

Introduction   7

Parenthood Ride   8

Chapter One: Neonatal Blues   15

Chapter Two: Fueling   61

Chapter Three: On Your Mark … Get Set …   85

Chapter Four: Grandparents   113

Chapter Five: Mom Stuff   135

Chapter Six: The Dadster   173

Chapter Seven: Hoo! Hoo! Hee! Hee! … AAAAUGH!   215
(Pregnancy and Delivery)

Chapter Eight: The Baby Blues Song Book   245

INTRODUCTION

About nine and a half years ago, a couple of old friends were looking forward to getting back together after about ten years spent in different parts of the country. These friends were cartoonists, and wanted to create a new comic strip together. The trouble was that one of the friends was about to become a dad for the second time, and this severely limited his availability. The other friend, confused by this thing called parenthood, waited patiently. Eventually, the two friends began to work on ideas for this new comic strip, but the first friend had trouble concentrating on anything but his new daughter. He would tell the second friend all about the joys, drudgeries, and horrors that babies bring . . . over and over and over again. He would describe the various noises, actions, and fluids that the child produced, the latter often accompanied by visual aids (his clothes). So fascinated was the second friend by this change in his pal that he actually sat and listened to this stuff. Eventually, the two gave up on the idea of developing a brilliantly innovative comic strip and created *Baby Blues* instead.

PARENTHOOD RIDE

(Sung to the tune of Don McLean's "American Pie")

It seems like long ago
I can still remember how our lifestyle used to be so wild.
And I knew that the time would come
When I would face the conundrum
of nature calling … me to … be a dad.

Then January made us shiver
We had a baby to deliver.
Stork was on the doorstep
We didn't want no forceps.

I felt so sorry for my bride
When I … finally saw … that head so wide.
But I just stood there flushed with pride
The first … time baby cried.

{Refrain}
So my, my, it's the Parenthood Ride.
Had our baby, and just maybe
We will feel qualified.
With colic and tears, the time just seems to rush by
I think this may be the way that I die
This could be the way that I die.

Did you read the book of Spock?
And do you agree it's all a crock
(Even though your mom says no)?
Do you believe in Brazelton?
Is Leach or Sears the wiser one?
Or do you have to learn this as you go?

Well I know that I've looked all around
And an owners manual can't be found.
We both just smile and shrug
Now we know why mom's so smug.

We were a D-I-N-K run amuck
Now it's clipping coupons just to save a buck
A big night out is now pot-luck
Wake up ... the baby's cry'n.

I started singin'
{Refrain}

Now for one year we've been overthrown
And talk gets done on a megaphone
But let's not speak of you and me.
When the Princess calls for her breast cuisine
In a tone that rivals a sirene
We soothed her with voices saccharine.

Oh, and while the kid was chowing down
We took our first chance to sit down
The mood was taciturn
No lesson had been learned!
And while laundry grew to heights unmarked
Our minds had lost their normal spark
So we just sat there in the dark
And then the baby cried.

We were singin'
{Refrain}

Helter Skelter, we ain't getting svelter
The kid crawls off leaving us to welter
Waistlines wide and growing vast.
Where did she learn to crawl so fast
I mean who could ever have forecast
That this baby could so quickly flabbergast.

Now we watch her first steps … oops! Kaboom!
As we raise the breakable heirlooms.
We worried in advance
Oh, but she had those padded pants!
We watched with pride so unconcealed
Mobility she had to wield
I can't describe just how we feel
We are preoccupied.

We keep on singin'
{Refrain}

Oh, and soon her toys were all misplaced
The living room a real disgrace
With no choice but to be chagrined.
So come on, back be nimble, back don't crick
Cleaning house ain't our bailiwick
'Cause tired is the state we're always in.

Oh, amorous urges we assuaged
And gambled with our parentage.
We heard the distant bell
The Round Two hammer fell.
Because the news we had to expedite
We rushed out fast into the night
We heard parents laughing with delight
The day the rabbit died.

We were singing
{Refrain}

Again this mother ate for two
And no snack or meal did she eschew
Oh, she just scarfed a Milky Way.
I went down to the corner store
Where they had the ice cream she adored
And the Ben and Jerry's sold out every day.
And time went past as in a dream
Excitement grew as it picked up steam
The child inside was pokin'
One night I was awoken.
With the three things we required most
A sitter, gas, and open roads,
We made it there with room to boast.
Another newborn cried.

And we were singin'

My, my, it's the Parenthood Ride
Had our babies, and just maybe
We will feel qualified.
With colic and tears, the time just seems to rush by
I think this may be the way that I die.
This could be the way that I die.

{Reprise}
We were singin'
My, my, it's the Parenthood Ride.
Had our babies, and just maybe
We will feel qualified.
With colic and tears, the time just seems to rush by
I want this to be the way that I die.

CHAPTER ONE
NEONATAL BLUES

The trouble with all babies is that they don't come with any sort of warning stickers, maintenance guides, or repair manuals. Of course, if they did, it would only make the birthing process that much more uncomfortable, so maybe it's just as well. The one thing that all first-time parents have in common is that they all believe theirs is the first child in recorded history to be so difficult/easy/colicky/sleepy/wakeful/quiet/loud/happy/sad/mad/glad or gassy. Which is good for us, because if there is a service we provide, it's showing people that they're not alone out there in the baby wilderness. There is a new certainty in the universe that if something bad has happened to you, it's probably worse for Darryl and Wanda.

This is the first Baby Blues® strip to appear in print. It's also the first and only time we broke our self-imposed rule about never allowing Zoe to think in words before she could speak.

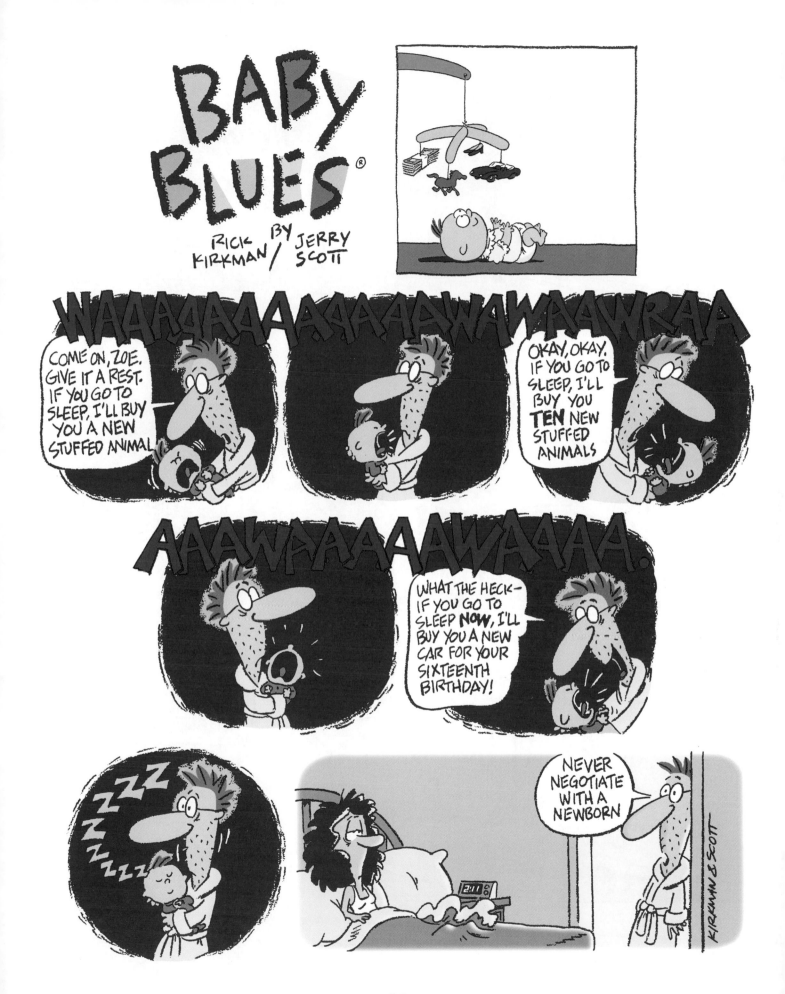

30

Darryl and Wanda's decision to use disposable diapers on Zoe caused a storm of controversy. We received lots of scoldings, lectures, charts, graphs, and articles supporting an argument against using disposables. Fortunately, we recycled those letters which made room in the landfill for the disposable diapers Darryl and Wanda would eventually use.

32

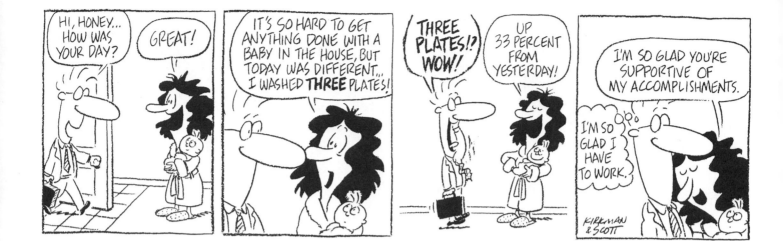

34

FAMILY PORTRAIT #1

45

KIRKMAN & SCOTT

WHEN I WAS PREGNANT WITH YOU I PLANNED TO TAKE SIX WEEKS OFF BEFORE GOING BACK TO WORK.

BUT AFTER YOU WERE BORN I EXTENDED IT TO TWELVE WEEKS... THEN SIX MONTHS... BECAUSE I KNEW YOU NEEDED ME.

-BIRP!

DO YOU SUPPOSE THERE'S SUCH A THING AS AN EIGHTEEN YEAR MATERNITY LEAVE?

KIRKMAN & SCOTT

OKAY, THEN IT'S SETTLED...

...IF YOU'RE NOT READY TO GO BACK TO WORK YET, WE'LL FIND SOME WAY TO MAKE IT.

I KNOW WE NEED THE MONEY, BUT WITH A NEW BABY, GOING TO WORK EIGHT HOURS A DAY, LIKE **YOU** DO, JUST DOESN'T SEEM RIGHT.

GOODNESS KNOWS I COULD USE THE REST, THOUGH...

VERY FUNNY.

KIRKMAN & SCOTT

HEY, WANDA...

AWWWWW... LOOK AT THAT FACE,

SO YOUNG...

SO FRESH...

SO INNOCENT...

KIRKMAN & SCOTT

WELL, SHE **WAS** JUST A FEW HOURS OLD...

I'M TALKING ABOUT **ME.**

CHAPTER TWO
FUELING

Early on in the development of *Baby Blues*, we decided that Wanda should breast-feed Zoe, and that we'd treat it as no big deal. Which, in itself is sort of a big deal, because we couldn't recall a comic strip in the past that has shown a woman discretely breast-feeding her child . . . let alone discussing the subject honestly. In the nearly eight years of syndication, we have had just one strip on this subject that one U.S. newspaper has refused to run (page 63, middle). That's probably why it's still our favorite.

Of course, breast-feeding is just the beginning. Once babies are weaned, things just get more interesting. There's something about the goopy, gloppy, viscous nature of most solid baby food that makes it such an irresistible subject for *Baby Blues*. Remember that TV commercial years ago for a super-adhesive where they glued that guy's hard hat to an I-beam and had him hanging from it? That's nothing. If they would have dabbed a little of the goo from the high chair tray of the average toddler on it, they could have dangled a hippopotamus from that hard hat!

A cartoonist has to work pretty hard to make another cartoonist laugh. That's where this strip started. Originally I slipped this fairly racy and nearly inappropriate gag into a regular batch of ideas just to make Rick laugh. Rick, of course got even by drawing the strip and giving it back to me as a part of a week's strips for my review. It struck us both as so funny that we decided to share the joke with our editor. So we included it with our regular group of strips that we sent to the syndicate, thinking she would laugh wildly and ask us for the milder replacement strip that we had already prepared. Which she would have certainly done if she hadn't been out sick that week. To make a long story short, the strip ran that week in papers all over the country with almost no outcry from newspapers or readers, and in fact has become one of the most popular strips we've ever done. Go figure.

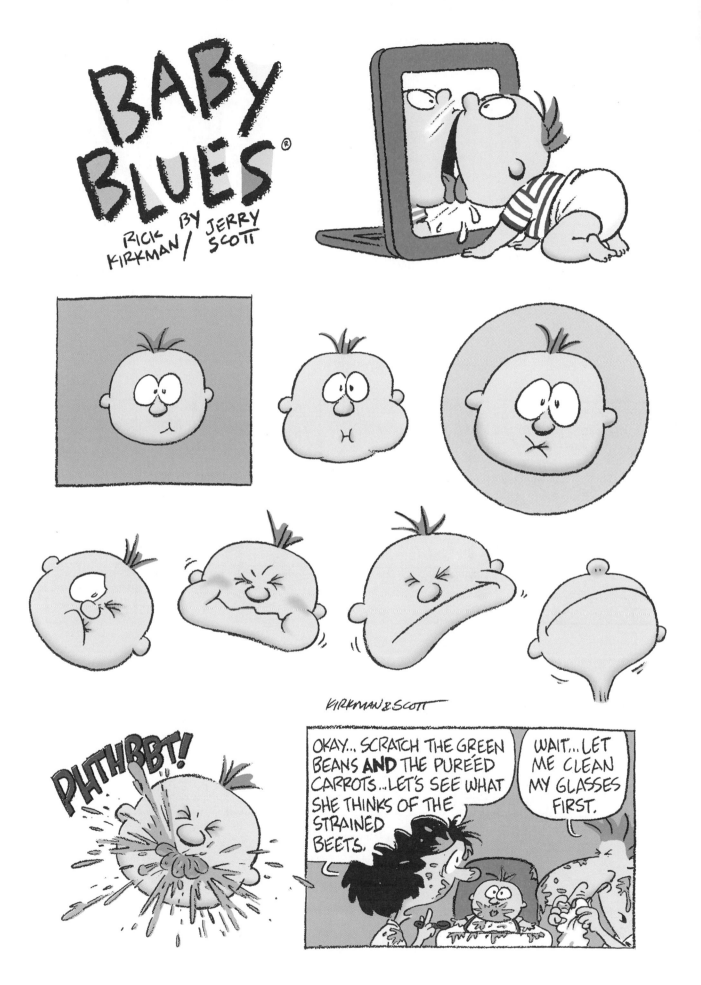

72

73

80

A lesson many of us learn early on in parenting is to think carefully before accepting food from a baby. This is a nearly verbatim account of one of Rick's early food encounters with his toddler.

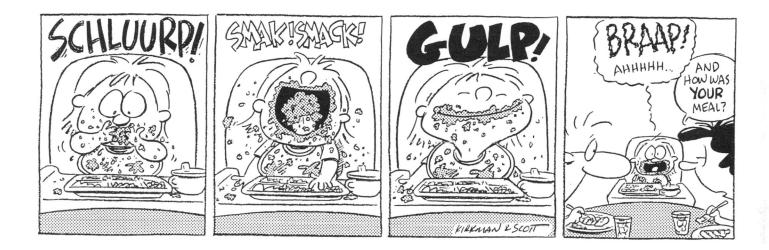

CHAPTER THREE
ON YOUR MARK . . . GET SET . . .

The day a baby rolls over for the first time is a milestone that marks the beginning of mobility for the child, and the end of anything resembling relaxation for the parents. From that moment on, one can never be completely sure where one's child is from nanosecond to nanosecond. No more setting the baby down while you fix dinner or take a moment for yourself. A crawling baby is an accident in search of a place to happen, causing parents to develop skills in watchfulness that put this country's defense systems to shame.

Zoe went through the usual stages when she learned to walk, but we've been having more fun with little Hammie. We heard somewhere that some kids learn to roll before they crawl, and some just skip crawling all together and go straight from rolling to walking. We thought this was a funny (if highly unusual image), so we made Hammie a roller. What has surprised us isn't the acceptance this has received, but the surprising number of letters from readers whose own kids are or were rollers! That's the great thing about kids . . . no matter how weird yours is, someone else's is bound to be weirder.

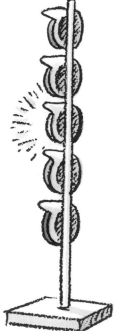

97

107

CHAPTER FOUR
GRANDPARENTS

Grandma … Grandpa … Grammy … Grampy … Meemaw … Peepaw … Ralph … Shirley … it doesn't matter what you call them. They're all the same. Grandparents (Latin for "revenge takers") play an important role in our lives and the lives of our children. Those of us who are lucky enough to have known our own grandparents remember what joy we felt during those times as kids when Grandma or Grandpa would openly defy or (better yet) secretly subvert some pointless ruling our parents made. Stupid rules, like no candy before dinner, or no driving until we were big enough to see over the steering wheel, begged to be broken, and all you needed was an adult ally. Grandpas usually relish this opportunity, but sometimes you end up with a really hip Granny who will possess an equally ornery side. But grandparents almost always take turns being the cool one because they know that if they're both fun to be with at the same time, there's the very real danger that the grandkids will want to visit *too* often. In fact, the threat of regular and frequent visits from the grandkids is the only weapon we parents have to control this behavior.

We decided that for maximum conflict in the strip, both Darryl's and Wanda's parents should be living, although very different people from each other. Wanda's parents are loosely modeled on Rick's in-laws, and Darryl's parents are somewhat like my mom and dad (notice the qualifying adjectives, *loosely* and *somewhat* … after all, they may be reading this chapter). So far, we're all still on speaking terms.

Kids and airplanes go together like Kool-Aid and white carpet. Naturally, we thought it would make the first trip to Grandma's a more complete experience if Darryl and Wanda could share their misery with a couple of hundred other people on the way.

117

Since they survived visiting Wanda's parents, the next test was to have Darryl's parents come to see baby Zoe.

119

In order for things to remain even, Wanda's parents came for Thanksgiving.

123

And just to keep Darryl and Wanda on their toes, we invited both sets of grandparents for Christmas.

THE GRAMCAM

127

"Road Trip." The only two words in the language that are guaranteed to strike terror in the heart of any parent.

CHAPTER FIVE
MOM STUFF

Is there any job in the world tougher than being a mother? Okay, being an alligator proctologist might be a *little* tougher, but the pay and benefits for that are probably pretty good. Not so with motherhood. Being a mom is a twenty-four-hour-a-day high-wire act with a flimsy net over broken glass. The responsibility is huge and the pay is non-existent. Plus, the reward for getting through a particularly rotten day in one piece is another day just like the one before it.

A lot of people ask us how we can write so sympathetically toward Wanda and issues of motherhood when we're just a couple of guys. We like to say it's because of our vast understanding of women and our warm, sensitive personalities. The truth is that almost all of the stuff that Wanda feels or experiences is stuff that our wives or friends felt or experienced first. We just sort of stand around and listen sympathetically. We may only be cartoonists, but we know what's good for us.

139

149

164

166

171

CHAPTER SIX
THE DADSTER

The definition of fatherhood has changed drastically during Darryl's life. He was born in the early sixties when a father was the undisputed head of the household. He grew up during turbulent changes in our society that suggested a father take a more permissive, "Do your own thing; I'm here if you need me, man" stance in his relationship with his children. Then came "The Involved Dad," "The Busy Dad," "The Guilty Dad," "The Back-To-Basics Dad," and "The Soccer Dad." Darryl seems to have absorbed all of these trends and attitudes and fashioned his own style of fathering, the "I Love My Kids Dad."

Being the father of two small kids just feels right to Darryl . . . or at least as right as anything can feel at three o'clock in the morning as you bring a drink of water to your child for the ninth time that night, or at four o'clock when you're changing the wet sheets. Darryl represents the pretty good dad in all of us guys . . . he's pretty patient, pretty calm, pretty resourceful, and pretty tired.

174

175

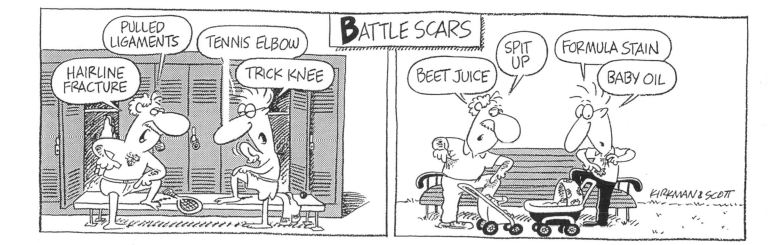

187

191

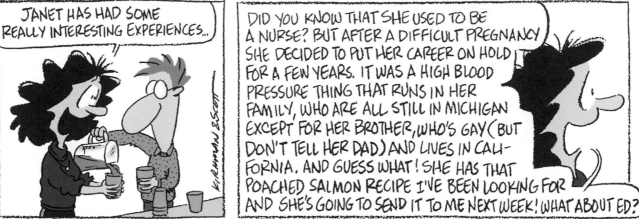

196

197

201

203

207

214

CHAPTER SEVEN
HOO! HOO! HEE! HEE . . . AAAAUGH!
(PREGNANCY AND DELIVERY)

No one was more surprised than us when Wanda found out she was pregnant for the second time. *Baby Blues* doesn't run according to some big master plan chiseled into a granite wall somewhere. It's more like, "Hey, wouldn't it be funny if . . .?"

Since the strip started just after Zoe's birth, we had never gotten the opportunity to go through a pregnancy and delivery with Wanda and Darryl. And because we began to sense a certain competency in their parenting, it seemed only right that we step in and add more chaos to their lives by giving them another baby. Who needs a comic strip in which the characters have things easier than its readers?

All the time she was pregnant, Rick and I debated whether Wanda would have a boy or a girl. Since both of us have daughters, it seemed only natural that Wanda should have another girl. Which is why she gave birth to Mr. Hamish MacPherson on April 29, 1995, after just fifteen short months of pregnancy.

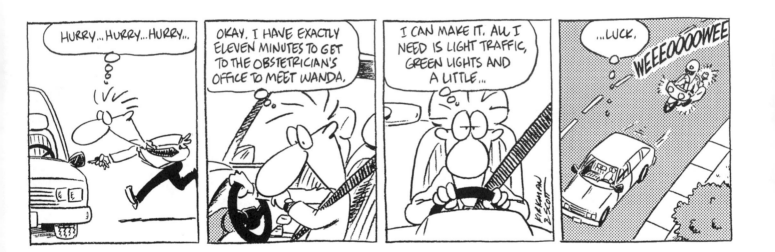

225

At this point, we were still debating the sex of the new baby. We eventually decided that Wanda would have a boy, so naturally we made them believe it was going to be a girl.

We probably went through half a dozen of those baby name books, and even had a contest in the form of a March of Dimes national fund-raiser. Even after we received thousands of name suggestions from that contest, we still didn't make up our minds until the last possible minute.

238

If you look re-e-e-e-ally close, you can see what we believe to be the first newspaper comic strip with an anatomically correct baby in it.

CHAPTER EIGHT
THE BABY BLUES SONG BOOK

Back in 1990, just as *Baby Blues* began in syndication, Billy Joel released an unusual hit song called "We Didn't Start The Fire." We were discussing the song at lunch one day, and wondered what it would be like to write something like that with such a huge complex, rapid-fire lyric. So we made the insane decision to parody the song in a Sunday strip. What sounded like a fun idea turned out to be three grueling days of listening to the song and rewriting the lyrics rhyme-for-rhyme and beat-for-beat. Our version is called "We Didn't Start Out Tired" and is one of the most popular *Baby Blues* Sunday strips we've created. No offense to Billy Joel, but if we never hear "We Didn't Start The Fire" again, it'll be too soon.

This chapter is a collection of all the songs we've parodied in the last seven years. Turn up the stereo, close the drapes, and enjoy.

WE DIDN'T START OUT TIRED
(SUNG TO THE TUNE OF BILLY JOEL'S "WE DIDN'T START THE FIRE")

BABY POWDER, BABY OIL,
RUBBER NIPPLES ON THE BOIL.
PACIFIER, VAPORIZER,
DOCTOR SPOCK IS BACK!

CHANGING TABLE, COTTON DIAPERS,
PAMPERS, HUGGIES, BABY WIPERS,
MIDNIGHT FEEDINGS, SUNRISE GREETING,
ARE WE HAVING FUN?

BASSINET, LAYETTE,
MASTERCARD JUST HAD A FIT.
BREAST FEEDING, BABY GNAWS,
TENDER NIPPLES, NURSING BRAS.

SOFT SPOT, CRADLE CAP,
CRANKY KID, I NEED A NAP!
HOUSECLEANING! INTERRUPTIONS!
NEVER GONNA GET DONE!

(CHORUS)
WE DIDN'T START OUT TIRED.
BUT WE THINK THAT MAYBE
WE CAN BLAME THE BABY.

WE DIDN'T START OUT TIRED.
IT SEEMS DIABOLIC
BUT IT'S PROB'LY COLIC.

246

TINY FINGERS, LITTLE TOES,
DIAPER RASH AND RUNNY NOSE.
BABY'S SHRIEKING, MILK IS LEAKING.
FIGURE IS SHOT!

PLAYPEN IN THE DEN,
BABY'S SLEEPING, AMEN!
PHONE RINGS, BELL DINGS,
IT MUST BE A PLOT.

COLIC, MYLICON,
WHERE THE HECK IS BRAZELTON?
CAMOMILE, FENNEL TEA,
DOUBLE SCOTCH FOR YOU AND ME.

WHITE NOISE, TAKE A RIDE,
VACUUM CLEANER, ALL TRIED!
ZOMBIE EYES, LULLABIES,
SINGING 'TIL WE'RE CROSS-EYED!

W (CHORUS)
E DIDN'T START OUT TIRED.
BUT WE THINK THAT MAYBE
WE CAN BLAME THE BABY.

WE DIDN'T START OUT TIRED.
BUT FOR THIS LITTLE ONE
OUR LOVE GOES ON AND
ON, AND ON...

(WITH APOLOGIES TO BILLY JOEL)

KIRKMAN & SCOTT

WHY'S SHE HAVE TO GROW?
   I SAY "WHOA!" (SHE WON'T OBEY)
I DON'T THINK IT'S WRONG
TO PROLONG THESE PRECIOUS
   DAY-AY-AY-AYS

YESTERDAY
THERE WEREN'T QUITE AS MANY
   BILLS TO PAY
WE HAD LOTS OF TIME TO TALK AND PLAY
BUT I WON'T TRADE FOR YESTERDAY

HMMM, MMM, MMM, MMM, MMM,
MM-MMMMM ZZZ ZZZ.

(WITH APOLOGIES TO PAUL McCARTNEY) KIRKMAN & SCOTT

CHILD THING

(SUNG TO THE TUNE OF THE TROGGS' "WILD THING")

GWAAAAA! CHILD THING!
YOU MAKE MY EARS RING!
YOU MAKE EVERYTHING —
DROOLEY!
CHILD THING!

(GUITAR) DAH-DER-DA-DERRR ♪♪
CHILD THING, I KNOW YOU'RE TEETHING...
DAH-DER-DA-DERRR ♪♪
AND I HOPE I CAN ENDURE!
DAH-DER-DA-DERRR
SO COME ON... SLEEP TONIGHT...
DAH-DER-DA-DERRR
I BEG YOU.

CHILD THING!
I KNOW YOUR GUMS STING.
I'VE GOT TEETHING RINGS—
COOOLIN'.
CHILD THING!

DAH-DER-DA-DERRR
CHILD THING, YOU NEED SOME NUMZIT...
DAH-DER-DA-DERRR
OR MAYBE YOUR ANBESOL!
DAH-DER-DA-DERRR
SO COME ON... SLEEP TONIGHT...
DA-DER-DA-DERRR
YOU **OWE** ME.

CHILD THING!
YOU TUG MY HEART STRINGS.
ISN'T **ANY**THING—
SOOOTHING?
CHILD THING!

COME ON, COME ON
CHILD THING...
HUSH UP, HUSH UP
CHILD THING...
TICKLE! TICKLE!
CHILD THING....

(WITH APOLOGIES TO THE TROGGS)
KIRKMAN & SCOTT

251

GRANDCHILD O' MINE!
SUNG TO THE TUNE OF JERRY LEE LEWIS' "GREAT BALLS OF FIRE"

YOU FRAY MY NERVES
  BUT I NEVER COMPLAIN
I GOT MORE LOVE
  THAN VARICOSE VEINS.
OH, WHAT A THRILL!
  YOU'RE SUCH A PILL!
GOODNESS GRACIOUS!
  GRANDCHILD O' MINE!

WE'LL PLAY ALL DAY
  TILL MY HAIR LOOKS FUNNY,
YOU SMILE AT ME
  AND YOU SWOOON ME, HONEY!
IT'S YOUR NAPTIME—
  I MUST RECLINE.
GOODNESS GRACIOUS!
  GRANDCHILD O' MINE!

KISS ME, BABY!
OOOO-MMM! FEELS **GOOD**!
HUG ME BABY!
WELLLL, I SPOIL YOU ROTTEN
   LIKE A GRANDMA SHOULD!
YOU'RE CRYIN'... I'M BUYIN'!
ANYTHING TO STOP
ALL THAT WHINE -
      WHINE-
         WHINE-IN'!

YOUR SCREAMS ARE LOUDER
THAN A HAND GRENADE,
DON'T NEED A BATTERY
   IN MY HEARING AID.
A TANTRUM'S NEAR—
   WE'RE OUTTA HERE!
GOODNESS GRACIOUS!
GRANDCHILD O' MINE!

WITH APOLOGIES TO HAMMER & BLACKWELL & JERRY LEE

HERE COMES THE SON

SUNG TO THE TUNE OF THE BEATLES' "HERE COMES THE SUN"

HERE COMES A SON (doo 'n doo-doo)
HERE COMES A SON,
AND I SAY, "IT'S A FRIGHT!"

LITTLE DARLIN', IT WAS A
SHOCK TO SEE YOUR GENDER!
LITTLE DARLIN', WE THOUGHT
A GIRL WAS TO APPEAR!

HERE COMES A SON (doo 'n doo-doo)
WE'RE BOTH SO STUNNED,
AND I SAY, "YOU'RE A SIGHT!"

LITTLE DARLIN', THE BLOOD'S
RETURNING TO OUR FACES.
LITTLE DARLIN', WE SEE THE YEARS
THAT YOU'LL BE HERE.

254

HE IS OUR SON.
LOOK WHAT WE'VE DONE.
AND I SAY, "HE'S JUST RIGHT."

SON, SON, SON, HERE WE COME!
SON, SON, SON-OF-A-GUN!
SON, SON, SON, HERE WE COME!
SON, SON, SON-OF-A-GUN!
SON, SON, SON, HERE WE COME!

LITTLE DARLIN', YOUR VERY
    FIRST SUNRISE IS DAWNING.
LITTLE DARLIN', IT'S JUST AN
    HOUR SINCE YOU GOT HERE.

HERE COMES THE SUN (doo 'n doo-doo)
WE HAVE A SON,
AND I SAY, "IT'S SO RIGHT!"

HERE COMES THE SUN (doo 'n doo-doo)
WE HAVE A SON.
IT'S SO RIGHT!
IT'S SO RIGHT!

(WITH APOLOGIES TO
GEORGE HARRISON)

KIRKMAN & SCOTT